E. Semmons.

A Little Wilderness

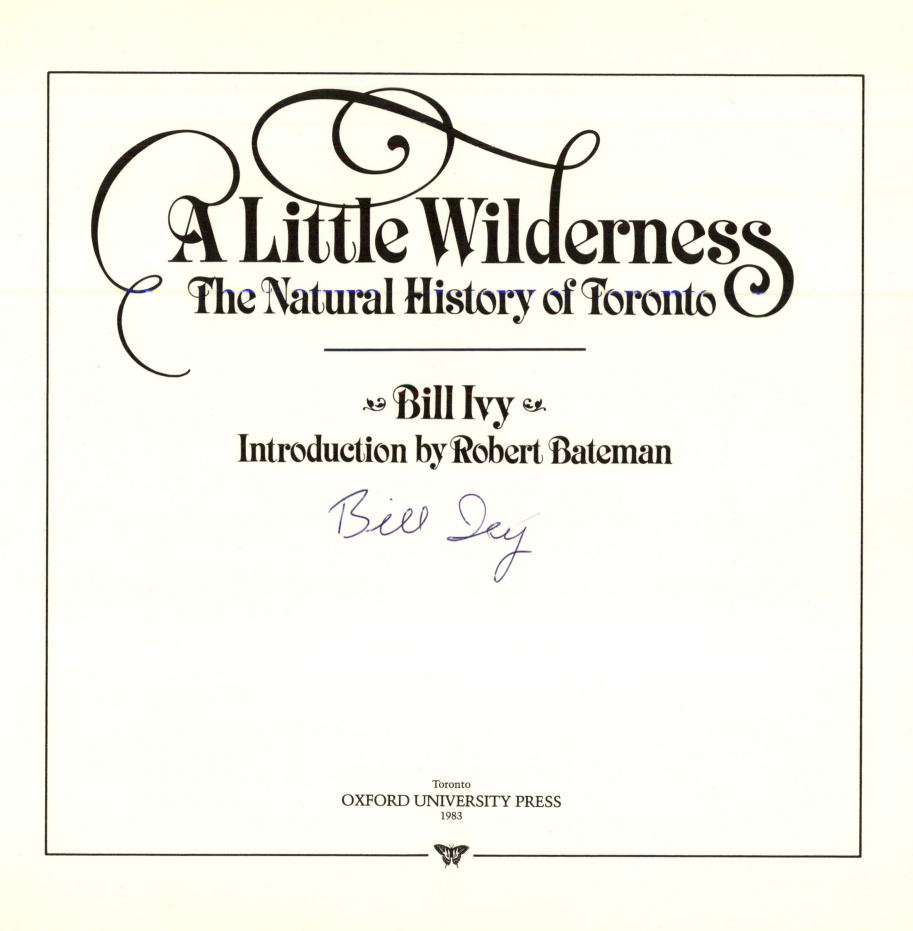

A Little Wilderness
The Natural History of Toronto

❧ Bill Ivy ❧
Introduction by Robert Bateman

Bill Ivy

Toronto
OXFORD UNIVERSITY PRESS
1983

For Patti Copeland

My thanks are due to the following people—
Nancy Azzarello, Robert Bateman, Roger Boulton,
Marjorie and Ray Francisco, Sally Livingston,
Roy Lucas, Rob Verner, Geordie, Jean, and Alan Zinn;
also to my parents, Lois and Jack Ivy.
Special thanks are due to Dr W.A. Jones and
Eric Nasmith for reviewing the text.

This book was published with the assistance of a
grant from the Toronto Sesquicentennial Board in
honour of the 150th anniversary of the City of
Toronto.

CANADIAN CATALOGUING IN PUBLICATION DATA

Ivy, Bill, 1953—
    A little wilderness: the natural history of Toronto

Bibliography: p. 135
Includes index.
ISBN 0-19-540421-1

1. Natural history—Ontario—Toronto Metropolitan Area.
2. Toronto Metropolitan Area (Ont.)—Description and travel.
I. Title.

QH106.2.05199   574.9713'541   C82-095335-0

Produced by Roger Boulton
Designed by Fortunato Aglialoro (Studio 2 Graphics)
Printed in Hong Kong by
Everbest Printing Company Limited

ISBN 0-19-540421-1

1 2 3 4 - 5 4 3 2

Introduction

When I was a boy in the 1930s, the bottom of our backyard was the entrance to a world as varied and exciting as any child could want. It was a ravine—a Toronto ravine; indeed the word 'ravine' is one that I have seldom heard used outside a Toronto context.

Our ravine was frequented by a steam engine, which puffed up and down twice a day, on a track that was called the Belt Line (because it encircled the upper part of Toronto like a belt) and provided a delivery service of coals for the furnaces and Lake Simcoe ice for the ice-boxes of North Toronto. As far as I could tell, the railway had no bad effects on the wildlife of the ravine. The train seemed to be simply another denizen of the place, and an exciting one, especially when the engine-driver shot off a burst of steam as we boys rushed away from the line after placing our pennies on the rails.

I would climb down into this inviting world over a low bank that my father had reinforced with cedar posts. Then I would find myself at the edge of a stream. The water was clear in those days and probably was still clear for another ten years or so after that—not that you would have drunk from it even then; but it was a real stream, a tributary of the Don, that flooded in spring and produced a wonderful variety of little creatures for one to capture, and learn about, and let go free again—minnows and pollywogs and even painted turtles. Today my stream is a storm sewer, buried underground, and the railway line has been replaced by a cinder track for joggers and cyclists.

The plant life in the ravine was fabulous and in many ways it still is. Our woods were a remnant of the beautiful mixed deciduous and coniferous forests *of maple, beech, ash, pine, and hemlock that covered the whole area in pioneer times; but because of the water level the dominant tree in our woods was the willow. Some of the largest willows that I have ever seen anywhere grew in our ravine. To a young lad they seemed like Amazonian giants. This jungly illusion was enhanced by a rampant growth of fox grapes and Virginia creeper that provided me with natural forts and castles.*

Every season was wonderful, but spring was the most exciting, with a gorgeous display of trilliums, trout lilies, hepaticas, and virtually every wild-flower of the deciduous woodland. I was a budding birder, however, and so for me the greatest treat of all was the spring migration. Often the birds crossing Lake Ontario would funnel up the Don and the Humber and their tributaries, the sea of surrounding buildings concentrating the birds into the ravines until it sometimes seemed as though our backyard was full to the treetops with birds. I remember one day sitting in a brilliant, fragrant bower of wild-plum blossom, waiting to see what birds would come to me. In less than an hour I was visited by many warblers and kinglets, and by a yellow-bellied sapsucker and a ruby-throated hummingbird. The very first year that I put up a nail-keg with a three-inch hole in it, as an 'owl barrel', in a burr oak in our front yard, sure enough, a pair of screech owls came and nested there.

For part of my youth I ran an early-morning Globe and Mail route that ended at Cedarvale Ravine, considered by all the birders to be one of the choicest vantage points in Toronto. I don't think I made any money on the route, but I certainly saw a lot of birds—including common loons flying over, and on one memorable morning white pelicans, in 'V' formation, sailing far up high against the blue.

I became a Junior Field Naturalist at the Royal Ontario Museum, and experts there like Jim Baillie and Terry Shortt opened my eyes to more distant and exotic havens of natural history in Toronto. By street car and on foot my birding buddies and I would go to Ashbridge's Bay for the great displays of arctic shore-birds and waterfowl that graced our city in the spring and fall. Another ambitious trip was to take the Queen car to the west end of the line, then to walk along Sunnyside Beach, through lower High Park, and so up the Humber Valley to Bloor Street. It would be a disappointing day in May if we did not see close to a hundred species of birds.

There may have been other cities with an equal abundance of handsome scenery and wildlife, but I know that I would never wish to exchange the Toronto of my childhood for any one of them. Much of the beauty of those early days is still to be seen around us even now, and I am very glad to find it portrayed in this book. Bill Ivy's work expresses something of the wonder in natural things that I and many others like me have experienced in Toronto down the years. I hope that this wild heritage will always remain a living part of our shores and marshes, woodlands and ravines.

ROBERT BATEMAN

Milton, Ontario
January 1983

I have a garden of my own,
But so with roses overgrown,
And lilies, that you would it guess
To be a little wilderness...
Andrew Marvell: *The Nymph Complaining*
for the Death of Her Fawn, 1681

Not so long ago, when Bloor Street from Avenue Road to Yonge Street was still a modest thoroughfare of two-storey buildings, with small stores at ground level and a floor of offices above, one could stand on the roof of the Park Plaza Hotel and look down on woodland. Only church spires, a few stone towers, university buildings, and the roofs of Yorkville poked up through the summer leaves. Far off, the heights of the upper Don Valley rose on the skyline through a peaceful haze. Avenue Road climbed through more trees to the Toronto Escarpment, accented on its ridge by Upper Canada College. To the south only a few tall buildings, such as the Royal York Hotel, interrupted the blue of the lake. There was little to hold the imagination from wandering across this vast surround of trees and waters and outlying fields to the open lands beyond.

It would be idle to labour the contrast between this and what we see today. In the course of a few years—two or three decades at most—the sprawling growth of Toronto has been tremendous. Our children will never remember this city as simply a pleasant town interwoven with its natural history and surroundings. They will accept the expressways and highrises as given features. They will find it hard to believe that their parents saw pheasants and herons, porcupines and foxes where bank towers and blocks of luxury condominiums stand. Instead of grumbling, then, the next time that raccoons dig up our newly sodded lawn, or we lug out another dozen bags of leaves from the ancient oak trees in the yard, or an indignant skunk makes us slam shut the bedroom window, perhaps we should stop to think how privileged we are to live in a city that even today allows us to have these links to its natural past.

Four hundred and fifty million years ago the region in which Toronto now stands lay submerged by a shallow sub-tropical sea.[1] Mountain ranges bordered it to the south and east. As these higher lands eroded, shale, limestone, silt, and dolomite were slowly deposited on the ocean floor. The sea retreated and the deposit became land surface, forming the bedrock of the region. (Some

[1] *Toronto the Green* (Toronto Field Naturalists' Club, 1976), p. 4.

of these rocks are visible today in the Humber Valley, and others have been exposed by excavation on the Don River.) Weathering and stream action eroded the bedrock, forming two deep valleys, one east of what today is the Humber River and another on the west branch of the Don. Drainage from Georgian Bay flowed south to form a stream in the basin left by the primeval sea. After the continental ice sheets had advanced across this region, layers of gravel, sand, and clay were laid by the meltwaters on the earlier bedrock below. These deposits are evident not only in excavations along the Don, but in the 120-metre (400-foot) heights of Scarborough Bluffs. Detailed study of this material suggests that three main periods of glaciation occurred 12,000 to 80,000 years ago. In the respites between the onslaughts of ice, the climate was much warmer than it is today, and plant life from mosses to large tropical trees flourished. Animal life included small marine creatures such as molluscs, and some larger vertebrates. As the glaciers advanced into low-lying areas, one tongue of ice pushed southwestward through the basin of Lake Ontario and another coming from the north pushed southward from the basin of Lake Huron. The Oak Ridges Moraine was formed between these two opposing masses of ice. Later a lake was created by meltwaters held between Lake Ontario, the Moraine, and the Niagara Escarpment. Thus clay of varying depths was laid on the glaciated plain, establishing the basis for fertile land in the still far-distant future.

As the ice was retreating, about 12,000 years ago, it blocked the bed of the St Lawrence valley and the meltwater deepened to form Lake Iroquois. The cliffs that formed the shoreline of this lake, about five kilometres (three miles) north of the present waterfront, are now the hills of Avenue Road and Yonge Street south of St Clair. To east and west, the deep valleys cut by the Don and Humber Rivers opened out into two great bays. Enormous sand and gravel bars were thrown across them by the waves and currents of Lake Iroquois. Then, as the ice-dam down in the St Lawrence valley melted, the waters of Lake Iroquois receded, allowing the rivers to extend their ravines further south.

By the time the ice had all gone, unblocking what is now the St Lawrence valley, the immense weight of the ice had so depressed the land that the sea poured in to invade the valleys of the St Lawrence, Ottawa, and Champlain-Hudson Rivers. Flowing on into the upper basin, this brackish water formed our present Lake Ontario. It was at this stage, when the sea level lay at the foot of Scarborough Bluffs, that wave action partially eroded the Bluffs to form sandbars off the river mouths. Eventually these sandbars joined to create a long peninsula which is now the Toronto Islands. Thereby a natural harbour came into being. With fertile land and a haven protected from the Great Lakes waters, the stage was set for man. It would

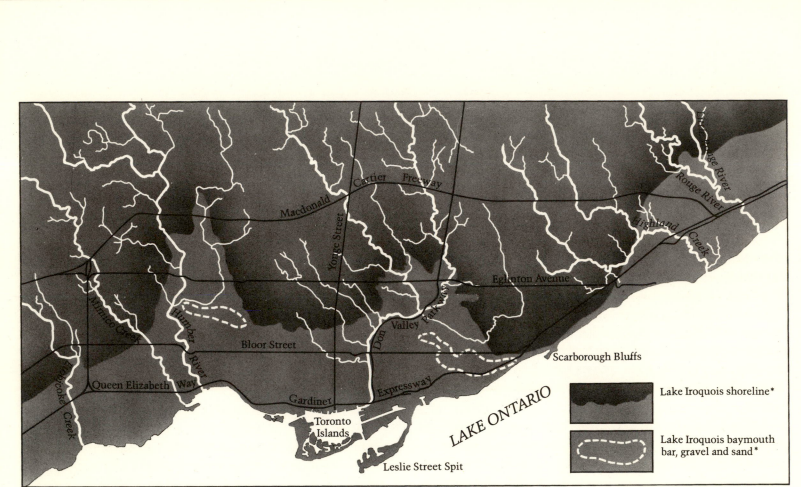

Lake Iroquois shoreline*

Lake Iroquois baymouth bar, gravel and sand*

* Bases: Ontario Division of Mines and Metropolitan Toronto and Region Conservation Authority.

still have to wait for his appearance, however—another eight thousand years.

On the retreat of the ice plants, birds, and animals moved north into the barren terrain. From 10,000 to 7,000 B.C., mastodons, elk, deer, caribou and giant beaver roamed the cool, post-glacial forests of spruce and fir. The finding of mastodon and mammoth bones along the sandbars of the lake suggests that these prehistoric creatures sought the windswept shores as refuge from the swarms of flies that must have infested the forests.

The earliest evidence of man dates from this period. Excavation has shown that mastodon hunters lived on the eastern end of Manitoulin Island about nine thousand years ago.[2] The first known humans in the Toronto area were the Lau-

[2]Robert R. Bonis, *A History of Scarborough* (Scarborough Public Library, 1965), p. 16.

rentian peoples, stone-workers who lived just east of present-day Toronto, from 3,000 to 1,000 B.C. These people were gradually replaced by an Iroquoian race from the southeast whose culture—which included pottery, tobacco, and the bow and arrow—may have survived until as late as A.D. 1,000. To the southwest lived another group of Iroquois, enjoying a milder climate and making a gradual transition from hunting and fishing to farming. Migrating into the Toronto area, they brought an economy based on corn, squash, beans and sunflowers. At one time the river valleys of the Rouge and Highland Creek supported a number of these people; but as soil nutrients and firewood became depleted, they moved further north, away from the heavy clay to higher and more fertile lands.

Arriving in the early eighteenth century, the first French traders and soldiers found dense and trackless forests lining the margins of the lake. Pure water flowed down the ravines to placid lagoons. The waterfront and the marshes of cat-tails, sedges, and reeds were the haunts of countless flocks of wildfowl. Yet it seems the region was more attractive to its wildlife than it was to some of its early European inhabitants. In 1793 E.A. Talbot described it as 'A piece of low marshy land which is better calculated for a frog pond or a beaver meadow than for the residence of human beings'. A few years earlier, in 1787, the Toronto Purchase from the Mississauga Indians had marked the beginning of modern times. After more than a century of varied and sporadic incursions by Senecas, Mississaugas, French and English traders and explorers, the period of continuous settlement was about to begin, with unforeseeable consequences for an environment which, until then, had remained virtually untouched and unchanged by man.

Half a century later, Toronto had developed into the trading centre of an expanding commercial region. Grist-, saw-, and woollen mills were built along the banks of the Humber and the Don; by 1860 there were ninety mills in operation on the Humber alone. Already industry had begun to take its toll. Waste from the mills was dumped into the rivers, and by 1895 the salmon had all but disappeared. As settlement spread, marshes and shallow ravines were filled in. Incalculable numbers of plants were uprooted, and much of the city's original wildlife was forced to flee north. Between 1885 and 1920 the city area increased fourfold. By the early 1960s nearly half the ravinelands had been destroyed, 340 hectares (840 acres) out of an original total of less than 800 hectares (2,000 acres).

The records of early settlement show this low swampy area to have been a scenic, if almost impenetrable, mixture of willow, poplar, and cedar trees, with thick, tangled undergrowth. Beyond lay unspoilt forests of butternut, beech, ash, oak, elm, maple, and the towering white pines for which the Don was once renowned. For many years these vast stands of timber provided the city with a flourishing lumber trade, but they were ravaged when the land was cleared for farm and pasture. In 1851 there were twenty-five saw-mills in what is now North York, yet by 1878 only eight remained. The wanton destruction and waste of the forest are well recorded. Wrote one observer: 'I have seen the best hardwood sold at a dollar a cord; great bonfires in which the best of pine, elm and maple were burning.' Some of the finest oak was split into rails to make 'snake fences'. Trees which had taken centuries to grow were rolled into log heaps and burned.[3] Many of Toronto's hemlocks were stripped of their bark for the tanneries, their timber gone to waste. A few sparse surviving remnants of red oak and white pine bear witness to what was once majestic forest.

Devastation of such a forest and its replacement by urban building might normally be expected to set in train the destruction of the region's entire wildlife system. That this has not yet been so in the case of Toronto, despite the grievous losses to which we shall later refer, must be largely attributable to its ravine and river systems. Until now, at least, these natural barriers have preserved flora and fauna that could not have survived in the usual twentieth-century urban environment.

Toronto's three major river systems are the Humber, the Don and the Rouge. Together they form a network of green space, woods, and parkland that reaches into the heart of the city. The Humber, once the main canoe route from Lake Ontario to Georgian Bay, is the largest river of the locality, with a drainage area of almost 57,000 hectares (220 square miles) and a main stream 100 kilometres (63 miles) long, running from the Niagara Escarpment near Mono Mills to Lake Ontario near the western outskirts of Toronto. The valley slopes of the Humber system are covered with a mix of deciduous trees and reach a depth of 30 metres (100 feet). In the 1790s there were eight marshes at the river's mouth. The five that remain today still support a great variety of plant and animal life.

Mimico and Etobicoke Creeks, on the western limits of the region, are much smaller than the Humber, but their names suggest their special place in Toronto's natural history. Mimico Creek derived its name from the Mississauga word meaning 'place of the wild pigeon': the forests surrounding it were once a favourite nesting site of the now extinct passenger pigeon. The name of Etobicoke Creek—'place where the alders grow'—recalls the time when extensive stands of these beautiful trees grew near its mouth.

The Don and its many tributaries drain an area of 37,000 hectares (132 square miles) in the central part of Metropolitan Toronto. Known to the Indians by various names (one of which—'black burnt lands'—indicates that the area was once scorched

[3]Charles Sauriol, 'Adventures in Tree Planting', *The Cardinal* 6 (Summer 1952) [Don Valley Conservation Association], p. 2.

by fire), the river was renamed by Lord Simcoe in memory of the Don in Yorkshire, England. Its headwaters rise from the coniferous woods of the till plain below the northern height of land to fall more than 240 metres (800 feet) over the total course before emptying into Lake Ontario. Along the way, cutting down 30 metres (100 feet) deep in some localities, the valley shelters willows and many native shrubs. (Each year, when the upper slopes are still covered in snow, the willows of the Don are among the first trees in the region to show their welcome clouds of colour, from the soft pink of swelling buds to the fragile greens of spring.) The river's principal branches, the East and West Don, converge on the main stream at the site of the former Lake Iroquois beach. The lower Don, like the Humber mouth, has been drowned by a rise in the level of Lake Ontario.

The eastern watershed of Toronto is drained by Highland Creek and the Rouge River. Shorter than either the Humber or the Don, Highland Creek has two branches, east and west, which meet in Morningside Park. Below this point the valley is deep and steep-sided as it flows downstream to meet Lake Ontario in the area of Scarborough Bluffs.

Meandering through the northeastern corner of the Metropolitan region, the Rouge River makes some of Toronto's most impressive scenery. In places, the valley's slopes rise for 45 metres (150 feet) above the river as it flows through stands of maple and hemlock. The Little Rouge is a major tributary running east of the main branch; its banks nurture sugar-maple, hemlock, white pine, and white cedar. One of the few surviving marshlands on the north shore of Lake Ontario is found at the mouth of the Rouge, providing a favourable habitat for various waterfowl, plants, and small aquatic animals. Between these two parallel rivers lies the Metropolitan Toronto Zoo, covering an area of 400 hectares (950 acres). The critical importance of this particular ecosystem can hardly be overstated. Although the two valleys are so steep that they have so far escaped development, the area and its wildlife—in particular a resident herd of deer—are now being threatened by plans for a housing project north of the Zoo. If the voice of caution and concern is ignored in this instance, the loss to future generations will be irreparable.

Spread out along the six major river valleys within the city are many public parks supporting a wide variety of plant and animal life. An integral part of Toronto's landscape, these parklands have survived largely because they are unsuitable for urban development. The rough, heavily wooded terrain along the narrow ravines is almost impossible for building, and the valleys too deep to fill; moreover there is the added danger of flash floods. Ironically, it was one of the most severe floods in the history of Toronto that led to much of the conservation effort that has preserved the ravines and parkland for us today. In the stormy fall of 1954, the normally placid rivers were swollen and their watersheds already saturated. On the evening of 15 October a torrential storm poured down an unprecedented 10 centimetres (4 inches) of water in the space of a few hours. The raging waters devastated everything in their path as they raced across the lowlands towards the lake. Hurricane Hazel had struck. In its wake it left eighty-one people dead and destruction amounting to a cost of $25 million.[4] Immediately afterwards the provincial government formed the Metropolitan and Region Conservation Authority to prevent similar destruction in the future. The Authority bought valleyland for flood control and turned it over to the Parks Department for management, beginning a progressive period of park development. By 1976 there were approximately 4,920 hectares (12,300 acres) of major valleyland park within Metropolitan Toronto. Once completed, the valleyland acquisition, as specified under the M.T.R.C.A.'s flood control and waterfront parks development plan, will eventually produce some 6,600 hectares (14,000 acres) of parks in the metropolitan area.

At present, many of Toronto's parks are attractively landscaped. Plans for future development, however, raise the question of whether such landscaping is really desirable. A growing number of people believe that these green spaces would be more valuable still if they were not 'developed' at all, but left in their natural state. The controversy over this question will no doubt continue for some time.

Toronto Island—originally a peninsula with sandy beaches, noble trees, and shallow lagoons bordered by rushes and wild rice—was frequently visited by native people who sought healing through the alleged curative powers of the place. Toronto's early European inhabitants used the area chiefly for fishing, hunting, and riding. In 1858 the peninsula was severed from the city by a violent storm that washed away a sandbar joining it to the mainland. It was granted in 1867 by the Crown to the city of Toronto, which then leased out the land. Centre Island, Hanlan's Point, and Ward's Island were developed into highly popular pleasure-grounds, containing hotels, amusements, two yacht clubs, and many summer residences. Approximately 320 hectares (800 acres) in area, 6.5 kilometres (4 miles) long and 150 metres (500 feet) wide, 'the Island' in fact consists of thirteen individual islands broken by a series of lagoons and channels. In 1954 they were taken over by the Metropolitan Toronto Parks Commission: the majority of the buildings were demolished (a small residential community on Algonquin and Ward's Island remained) and most of the acreage was turned into parkland. Until the building of the Outer Harbour (a man-made spit) the Island was growing at the rate of roughly half a metre (2 feet) per year. Now, unfortunately, erosion is taking its toll.

[4]Bruce West, *Toronto* (Toronto: Doubleday Canada Ltd., 1979), p. 233.

As in time the Island became more and more popular for recreation, so the environment and the wildlife began to suffer. Thanks to the efforts of the Toronto Field Naturalists' Club and the Federation of Ontario Naturalists, however, restrictions were established to discourage casual visitors from vulnerable areas, while allowing those with a serious interest to study the Island's wildlife.

The Island's strategic location has always attracted a diversity of wildlife, making it a favourite haunt of bird-watchers. Common spring and autumn migrants gather in large numbers on and off its shores, and occasionally rare sightings are reported as well. Geese, gulls, and pheasants are among the larger year-round residents, and many smaller year-round birds nest in the trees and shrubs. In order to track their movement and record population changes, bird-migration monitoring programs have been set up on the Island by the Toronto Bird Observatory, where thousands of birds are banded and recorded annually. During the spring of 1981 one hundred and twenty-five different species were identified,[5] while 1,244 birds of seventy-seven species were banded. Moreover, this site is famed as a stop-over point for migrating saw-whet owls, as many as forty-five having been sighted on a single October day.

One of the greatest contributions to the welfare of Toronto's wildlife in recent years was the building of the Leslie Street Spit, also known as the Eastern Headland. Starting out from the foot of Leslie Street, this 4.8-kilometre (3-mile) long piece of landfill jutting into the cold waters of Lake Ontario was begun by the Toronto Harbour Commission as long ago as 1959. The headland was originally meant as a harbour extension, an aim which was never met. Although completed by 1972, the Spit was not officially opened to the public until the following year. Shortly after its completion gulls, terns, herons and geese began to arrive, as sparse vegetation appeared. The Spit's 100 hectares (250 acres) of meadowland, edged by a series of bays and lagoons, have since become a haven for birds. In just over two years more than forty different species were recorded and this number has by now risen to over two hundred.[6] As well as immense colonies of nesting gulls and terns, many shore-birds, raptors, warblers, and songbirds are to be found here over the course of a year. Each winter, on the waters around the Spit, warmed by Ontario Hydro's Hearn Generating Station, about thirty different kinds of waterfowl can be seen. The future of the Leslie Street Spit is now the subject of heated debate. Realizing the importance of keeping the Spit as a wildlife sanctuary, the city's naturalists want it left alone and undeveloped. Other groups see the Spit as an ideal place for a park and recreational sports such as sailing and boating. It remains to be seen if the interests of

[5]Bruce D. Parker, 'News from the Toronto Bird Observatory', *Toronto Field Naturalists' Newsletter* no. 342 (October 1981), p. 4.

[6]Don Sedgwick, 'The Spit', *Seasons*, Spring 1980, pp. 45–7.

wildlife preservation will prevail.

Toronto's southern location, moderate climate, adequate rainfall, and variable soil enable it to support a wide range of flora. Situated on the border of two merging life zones—the Southern Hardwood region (Carolinian zone) and the Great Lakes Forest region (Alleghanian zone)—the area displays abrupt changes in vegetation. An example of this is the western part of the city, notably High Park, where one can still see trees characteristic of the Carolinian zone (hemlock, sugar maple, and beech) in the bottom of the deep ravines to the east.

Centuries of change have brought about such a confusing mixture of plants that historical study of the city's vegetation is difficult. We cannot judge from existing trees what the original forests were, since when one species has been destroyed by fire or disease, it is usually replaced by secondary growth of entirely different species. Another complication is that species not native to the region have been introduced and kept in continuous cultivation. Some trees associated with the southern United States have spread into Toronto as secondary growth. Among these are the chestnut, black walnut and sassafrass, which here reach the northern limit of their distribution. Other species such as the turkey, pin, and pedunculate oaks, shagbark hickory and cucumber tree, are rare in the region and need protection. Rarer still are the sweet chestnut, pignut hickory, and hackberry, with

fewer than three specimens of each remaining in Metropolitan Toronto.[7]

The first wildflower to appear is the skunk cabbage, which often protrudes out of lingering snow patches in early March. Soon bloodroot, spring beauty, and dog-tooth violet open to the sun, and colour slowly returns to the land. The umbrella-like leaves of May-apple and trillium (both purple and white) carpet shady woods and slopes, where blue and yellow violets, squirrel corn, dutchman's breeches, and herb Robert can also be found. In moist ravines grow marigolds, jack-in-the-pulpit, and many ferns (Toronto has roughly a dozen)—often in profusion. As the spring flowers fade, buttercup, jewelweed, goldenrod, and butter-and-eggs appear, bringing the city to full bloom. Before long the wild fruit—red and black raspberry, strawberry, chokecherry and blackberry—will ripen.

As in the case of the trees, it is difficult to identify Toronto's indigenous plants. Many non-native varieties have been introduced—sometimes intentionally, sometimes accidentally—in the course of urban development, including such familiar species as the dandelion, day lily, chickory, coltsfoot, Queen Anne's lace, ox-eye daisy and stinging nettle. Where patches of natural terrain remain undisturbed, a few unusual plants can still be found. The richest area of this kind can be found in the lower Rouge River marshes, which contain

[7] Mary Smith, 'More About Heritage Trees', *Toronto Field Naturalists' Newsletter* no. 345 (February 1982), p. 27.

thirty-one regionally rare plants, including the bluejoint grass, bushy cinquefoil, lake sedge, and wild lupine.[8] The fertile environment of such marshes is essential both for these rare species and for more common flora. Tragically, however, the wetlands of Toronto have nearly all been destroyed. About eighty-nine per cent of the local marshlands have now been lost either to housing, industry, marinas or ports.[9] Only an attitude of active concern can save the unique floral displays of the few marshes that remain.

Because it not only combines a lakefront with both evergreen and deciduous habitats, but is on a major migration route, Toronto offers refuge to a vast array of birds. The largest influx occurs in spring and fall when, given the proper conditions, over one hundred species may be observed in one day. Red-winged blackbirds, robins, killdeer, Canada geese, and woodcocks are the earliest harbingers of spring, arriving from warmer climes in March. By the end of April the belted kingfisher, white-throated sparrow, barn swallow, and kinglets have arrived. May is the month for warblers, with the black and white, the yellow-rumped and the pine usually among the first to be seen. By the middle of June the spring migration has ended and some of the seventy-five species that nest in Toronto have already begun to incubate their eggs.

Among the more notable nesters are the great horned owl, screech owl, red-tailed hawk, kingfisher, ring-necked pheasant, indigo bunting, and scarlet tanager. Leslie Street Spit shelters one of the largest nesting colonies of gulls and terns on the Great Lakes—the only one in fact where the ring-billed gull population is on the increase. Each year more than 60,000 pairs of ring-bills, hatching an estimated 120,000 eggs, nest here, along with thousands of common terns and a number of Caspian terns and herring gulls.[10]

With the approach of autumn, the city's bird population swells once again as thousands of migrants continue their journey south. Many species that once migrated now winter in the Toronto region, partly because there is more food available. The regional bird censuses taken throughout the year by both the Toronto Field Naturalists' Club and the Federation of Ontario Naturalists have contributed greatly to our knowledge of the city's bird-life. The annual Christmas counts record as many as eighty species of birds, while about twenty-four species of waterfowl numbering over 20,000 individuals are counted each January.[11] Winter residents on the waterfront include the Canada goose, mute swan, mallard, redhead, oldsquaw and black duck, while woodlots throughout Metro support a welcome variety of

[8]Steve Varga, 'Rare Plants of the Lower Rouge Valley', *Toronto Field Naturalists' Newsletter* no. 333 (September 1980), p. 15.

[9]*Ibid.*

[10]Clive Goodwin, quoted in George Gamester, 'Gulls with Gall', *Toronto Star*, 27 May 1982, p. A2.

[11]*Toronto the Green*, p. 7.

species, including the black-capped chickadee, cardinal, blue jay, white-breasted nuthatch, goldfinch, mourning dove, and dark-eyed junco. Surprisingly the robin, a bird usually associated with the spring, now chooses to winter here in growing numbers—in 1981 the total was estimated at one thousand. House sparrows and rock doves (pigeons) of course have adapted particularly well to city life, and are abundant in most areas throughout the year.

Rarities are exciting at any season. In 1981 a wild sandhill crane selected the Toronto zoo as a winter retreat and on 11 September 1981 a gray flycatcher was banded and released on Toronto Island, a first for Canada. Other less common winter sightings include the snowy and long-eared owls, pileated woodpecker, hoary redpoll, kingfisher, and northern shrike. In recent years keen year-round birders have reported such unusual species as the blue-throated gray warbler, blue grosbeak, Townsend's solitaire, and blue-winged warbler.

As Toronto's suburbs have grown, the city has witnessed a proportionate decline in its mammal population. Formerly, timber wolves, minks, ermines, bears, and martens roamed the woods and ravines. In the early 1800s there were occasional reports of bears and wolves preying on the farmers' livestock; indeed, legend has it that Bay Street was for a while known as 'Bear Street', after the celebrated Mr Justice Boulton's horses attacked a bear in the vicinity. This abundance of wildlife was a bountiful resource for the early fur traders, who pursued the beaver in particular almost to extinction. Many smaller species once common in the area have long since disappeared. In *The Natural History of the Toronto Region* J.H. Faull shows that, as late as 1913, the prairie cottontail, jumping mouse, flying squirrel, masked shrew, silver-haired, and red-backed bats could still be found, but other species such as the northern Virginia deer, red-backed mouse, fisher and southern varying hare were already gone.

Although few animals can survive the congestion, the pollution, and the subsequent drop in food supply caused by the growth of a city, some hardy species have managed to adapt. A few even seem to thrive in this drastically altered environment. The raccoon, striped skunk, eastern gray squirrel, brown rat, and house mouse, for example, seem not in the least intimidated by man. A far greater number of species, however, prefer the more secluded settings on the borders of residential areas. In these enclaves of relative peace and quiet may be found the muskrat, cottontail rabbit, groundhog, red squirrel, eastern short-tailed shrew, star-nosed mole, meadow vole and eastern chipmunk, as well as their sometime predator, the red fox, an elusive resident which raises its kits in a few select valleys and is careful to avoid any meeting with man. Surprisingly, white-tailed deer and coyote may still sometimes be found in certain parts of the Rouge River Valley, although their future is threatened by urbanization.

From time to time stragglers from the north come into the city. In January 1968 a Canada lynx was seen in a northwest suburb—the last previous documented sighting was in the early 1900s, and at that time the animal was considered a migrant.[12] As recently as the summer of 1981 a moose ventured into the Rouge Valley; unfortunately police found it necessary to shoot the bewildered beast.

Toronto's reptile and amphibian population is gradually shrinking. Approximately half of the species that once lived here have left, primarily because their preferred habitats—bottomland woods, meadows, and marshes—have disappeared. These cold-blooded animals hibernate under soil, rocks, or water until, from the scattered wetlands, the distinctive calls of spring peepers, western chorus frogs, and Canadian toads signal the commencement of spring. As the ground slowly thaws, snakes begin to stir; the most common is the eastern garter snake, often seen in the gardens of suburban homes. The deKay's, eastern milk, and northern water snakes also inhabit Toronto, but in lesser numbers. Although the black rat, smooth green, hog-nosed, ring-necked, and riband snakes have all apparently left the region, it is thought that the seldom-seen red-bellied snake (which has never been common) still lives here. Also active but rarely seen are the red-backed sala-

mander and red eft (eastern newt). The spotted salamander, which once dwelt in woods throughout the city, has all but disappeared.

In a few woods adjacent to wetlands, the trilling call of the gray tree-frog is still heard in early summer. Green, leopard, and wood frogs still frequent similar habitats, but most of the species found here in earlier days—including the bullfrog, swamp tree, cricket, pickerel, and Cambridge frogs—have vanished.

On the banks and logs of isolated ponds both snapping and painted turtles may be seen basking leisurely in the summer sun, and the mainly terrestrial wood turtle is sometimes spotted in moist shady woodlands. The uncommon inhabitants are the wood turtle, the stinkpot, and the Blanding's turtle—an endangered species which may have been reintroduced to Toronto. The map, spiny softshell, and spotted turtles, however, have presumably failed to survive here, and it is obvious that unless some measures are taken to reverse past trends, Metro's reptile and amphibian population will continue to decline.

The once-crystalline waters of Toronto used to abound in whitefish, salmon, black bass, perch, pike, brook-, lake-, and speckled trout. Today fourteen species of game fish and several small fry can still be found in the lower Rouge River;[13] however, in most places extensive pollution by heavy industry has either killed or driven away all but the

[12]J.H. Faull, *The Natural History of the Toronto Region* (Toronto, The Canadian Institute, 1913), p. 211.

[13]Varga, p. 15.

hardiest fish. Among the few survivors are the chub, sucker, carp, and stickleback. Some attempts have been made to restore the city's aquatic population. Grenadier Pond in High Park, for example, has been successfully restocked with a variety of fish.

Insects are by far the most numerous of Toronto's wild inhabitants, and no wonder: it is estimated that there are over 100,000 species of insects in North America alone. Generally unappreciated by man, they display a tremendous diversity of colour, size, and shape, varying from the bizarre to the beautiful. Moreover they constitute an essential link in the food chain, as staple nourishment for innumerable birds, reptiles, and smaller mammals. Unquestionably the best-loved insects are the butterflies, which frequent most of the city's fields, marshes, woods, and backyard gardens. Though still fairly common, these exquisite creatures were once far more abundant. In 1796 Mrs Simcoe observed 'millions of yellow and black butterflies dancing and flying about' in a meadow at the site of the present Don Valley Brickyards. Today about sixty species of butterflies exist in the region.[14] Many of these are well known, particularly the tiger swallowtail, yellow sulphur, cabbage white, and monarch. Unlike the monarch, which migrates, several species winter in the city at various stages of their growth. Adult

[14]Bill Edmonds, 'Some Butterflies of Toronto', *Toronto Field Naturalists' Newsletter* no. 341 (September 1981), p. 7.

mourning cloaks, red admirals, tortoise-shells, and angelwings, for example, seek refuge from the winter cold under the bark of trees, or in other suitable crevices.

The butterflies' closest relatives, the moths, are even more widely represented in Toronto. The majority may be rather unimpressive, but some are quite striking, and the giant silk moths— Cecropia, Polyphemus and Promethea—are among the grandest insects anywhere. Though not uncommon, these are seldom seen, because of their short lifespan and nocturnal habits.

All the species of flora and fauna portrayed in this book can be found and photographed in Toronto. Surprising though some of them may be even to a naturalist, their presence at this time can be verified by reference to the sources listed in the bibliography and from my own experience. (Locations have not been given except in general terms, in order that vulnerable and sometimes endangered species should not be put at risk.) Clearly, Toronto has inherited a priceless legacy of flora and fauna. It is amazing that such a significant body of wildlife has managed to survive in the midst of a metropolis of over two and half million people. What is true for every city is true here also; past apathy and ignorance have been costly and our natural areas and their inhabitants face a perilous future. Fortunately our society is slowly becoming more sensitive to the need for conservation; governments are under increasing pressure from concerned citizens and conservation groups to enforce controls on pollution and land development. Though Toronto's atmosphere and its rivers are still polluted, there is reason for optimism in this respect also. It is not too late to undo much of the damage that has been done. One case in point is the Don River. During the 1950s the lower Don may well have been the most severely contaminated river in Ontario, considering its small volume of flow.[15] However, the 1960s saw a determined effort to make the Don biologically safe and as a result its water quality has notably improved. Nevertheless, much of Toronto's natural heritage is beyond recall. The evidence of our loss is apparent in the work of the many naturalists, writers, and artists who have been attracted to Toronto from its beginnings—among them Paul Kane, Ernest Thompson Seton, J.E.H. MacDonald, and Tom Thomson. The untamed beauty that delighted their eyes and inspired their imaginations is gone forever.

My own observations as a naturalist confirm a marked decline in the city's wildlife, native trees, and plants over the past ten years. To preserve what remains will require that we provide a healthy environment. Disease, overcrowding, and other such pressures can be devastating. If these are not to eliminate our wildlife altogether, the natural areas that remain must not be isolated from the hinterland. It is absolutely essential that wildlife corridors be left intact, forming a continuous network of green spaces leading to the countryside beyond. As the spread of suburban building shuts off the northern ends of the ravine systems, there is a real danger that the wildlife trapped in the city will fall prey to fatal epidemics. The channels that allow animals to move, redistributing themselves according to available food supplies and living space, must be preserved and kept open.

These natural areas are equally important to the city's human population. Green spaces refresh the very air we breathe; moreover, they offer both rest and aesthetic relief from our sterile urban surroundings. Unlike most of the world's great cities, Toronto has had the good fortune to keep a few precious links to the natural world—a reminder, and at the same time a promise, of what we can enjoy if only we treat our surroundings and their natural inhabitants with compassion and concern. In the hope that others will both share in their beauty and care for their future, this book is dedicated to all the wild living things of Metropolitan Toronto.

BILL IVY

Toronto, January 1983

[15]Forbes Gilbertson, 'The Don: An Urban River Struggling for Survival', *Canadian Geographic Journal*, February 1972, p. 67.

Captions to plates 1–12

1–2 RED FOX *Vulpes vulpes*

Seldom seen, this elusive ravine inhabitant has earned a reputation for cunning. Its average lifespan is a short three years, during which time pairs are thought to remain monogamous. Breeding takes place in the winter, and by March or April from four to nine kits are born in a den lined with grasses and leaves. The fox's varied diet includes insects, mice, rabbits, groundhogs, and berries. The male, or dog fox, does the hunting for the family until late summer, by which time the young must learn to fend for themselves.

3 Scarborough Bluffs at dawn

4 SHOWY LADY'S SLIPPER *Cypripedium reginae*

With its waxy-white petals and generous pink pouch, the showy lady's slipper is undoubtedly Canada's most spectacular native orchid. Nearly a metre (36 in.) high, it blooms from May to August in bogs, swamps, and wet woods. Unfortunately, as a result of overpicking and the destruction of wetlands, very few plants survive in the Toronto region.

5 FLOWERING RUSH *Butomus umbellatus*

Originally from Eurasia, this showy member of the rush family blooms from July to September in shallow muddy ponds, ditches, and slow-moving streams. The umbrella-like cluster of lavender-pink flowers, each growing on its own stem, is displayed atop a sturdy stalk 60 to 100 cm. (24 to 40 in.) tall. Although this plant is well established along the Great Lakes shoreline and in the St Lawrence valley, it is not common in Toronto.

6 CARDINAL FLOWER *Lobelia cardinalis*

This striking scarlet member of the bluebell family colours eastern woodlands, swamps and streambanks. It is the only red lobelia, the others being blue or white. A 60 to 120 cm. (2 to 4 ft) perennial, it blooms from July to September, attracting hummingbirds which act as pollinators. The cardinal flower is rare in Toronto, having suffered from overpicking, and is now a protected species.

7 CARDINAL *Richmondena cardinalis*

The earliest record of a nesting in Toronto dates from 1922. Now well established, this year-round resident feeds mostly on seeds, many of which are provided by backyard feeders. The brilliant scarlet plumage of the male is not shared by the predominantly olive-brown female. Often seen together, the pair raise three or four young in a loosely constructed nest of twigs, grass, and bark built fairly close to the ground in gardens, thickets, and woodland edges.

8 EVERLASTING PEA *Lathyrus latifolius*

Closely resembling the domestic sweet-pea, this pretty perennial is a garden escape introduced from Europe. Its 3.8 cm. (1½ in.) flowers, which bloom from June to September, vary greatly in tone, from hot pink to pale blue or white. A hardy species with an extensive root-system, it favours river-banks, roadsides, and waste places, where it often serves to reduce soil erosion.

9 PASTURE ROSE *Rosa carolina*

The wild rose, a prickly shrub found in open woods and rock pastures, belongs to the large family 'Rosaceae', which includes raspberries, strawberries, peaches, and cherries. Its fragrant pink flowers bloom in May and June, but soon fade and are easily damaged. The red seed-pods, or hips, make a tasty jam, as well as the popular rose-hip tea.

10 EASTERN CHIPMUNK *Tamias striatus*

This alert member of the squirrel family is primarily a ground-dweller, feeding on nuts, seeds, and small invertebrates. While gathering food, it makes countless trips to its burrow, where it stores up to half a bushel of food for the winter. Born in April in a litter of from three to six young, the chipmunk has an average lifespan of three years, during which time it will seldom leave its small territory (roughly one hectare, or two to three acres).

11 RED SQUIRREL *Tamiasciurus hudsonicus*

The typical red squirrel inhabits a small home range—usually no more than 200 m. (700 ft) across—in a mixed coniferous and hardwood forest. Highly territorial, it will defend its winter food cache—as much as ten barrels' worth—aggressively. Its varied diet consists of twigs and buds, seeds, mushrooms, birds' eggs, and insects. In spring and early fall, from two to seven young are born in a leaf nest or hollow-tree den, and six weeks later they venture outside for the first time. Early broods scatter by autumn, but later families winter together. Although they do remain in their dens during extreme weather conditions, they do not hibernate.

12 BLOODROOT *Sanguinaria canadensis*

As the name suggests, the rootstalk and stem of this delicate plant contain an orange-red juice. This sap—which is toxic—provided Indians and early settlers with a versatile dye and mosquito repellant. Bloodroot uncurls its broad leaves and flowers in early spring. As with most members of the poppy family, its beautiful blooms are short-lived, and the slightest disturbance will cause them to fall.

1 RED FOX

2 RED FOX

3 SCARBOROUGH BLUFFS AT DAWN

4 SHOWY LADY'S SLIPPER

5 FLOWERING RUSH

6 CARDINAL FLOWER

7 CARDINAL

8 EVERLASTING PEA

9 PASTURE ROSE

10 EASTERN CHIPMUNK

11 RED SQUIRREL

12 BLOODROOT

Captions to plates 13–24

13 COMMON GRAY TREE FROG *Hyla versicolor*

This amphibian is seldom seen except when it is breeding in quiet shallow ponds and streams. Once its eggs are laid it returns to the seclusion of a high tree where, clinging by means of the large adhesive disks on its feet, it feeds on various small insects. Its colour and pattern vary with the light, temperature and setting, providing remarkable camouflage, but its loud, trilling call is an unmistakable field mark.

14 LARGE-FLOWERED TRILLIUM
  Trillium grandiflorum

A protected species, Ontario's floral emblem is the largest of the trilliums. The flower measures 5 to 10 cm. (2 to 4 in.) across, and the plant itself may reach a height of 45 cm. (18 in.). It blooms in shady woodlands throughout Ontario and Quebec from March to May.

15 MOURNING CLOAK *Nymphalis antiopa*

Thought to have been named after the dark shawls worn by widows, the elegant Mourning Cloak has a wingspan of up to 8 cm. (3³/₈ in.). After a winter of hibernation in the adult stage, it is one of the first butterflies to appear in early spring and can often be seen flying over lingering snow patches.

16 BLACK-CAPPED CHICKADEE *Parus atricapillus*

The distinctive black cap and bib found on both the male and the female quickly identify the chickadee. Only 12 to 14 cm. (roughly 5 in.) long, it is noted for the agile acrobatics it displays in pursuit of insects and wild fruit. Chickadees are permanent residents of southern Canada, and rove through mixed woods and backyards in loosely organized groups, unperturbed by the coldest weather. Its cheery call—'chick-a-dee-dee-dee'—has given the species its name.

17 POINTED BLUE-EYED GRASS
  Sisyrinchium angustifolium

This dainty member of the Iris family, a native of North America, can be found in meadows from coast to coast. It is an extremely variable species, with a flower that ranges in colour from white, yellow or pink to violet-blue. Supported on a grass-like stem, it blooms for one day only (in May or June) and is therefore easily overlooked.

18 Misty pond, Brookbanks Ravine

19 GREAT BLUE HERON *Ardea herodias*

Canada's most widely distributed heron, the majestic great blue heron, once hunted for its head-plumes, is now a protected species. Its diet consists mainly of aquatic animals, but may also include insects and small rodents. Although most great blue herons migrate for the winter, some do remain in Canada, though not all survive the cold.

20 BLUE FLAG *Iris versicolor*

An eight-spotted forester moth *(Alypia octomaculata)* accents the beauty of this flower's delicate purple-veined sepals. Sometimes several such blooms will appear on a single stalk. A member of the Iris family, the blue flag blossoms from May to July in wetlands.

21 SHARP-LOBED HEPATICA *Hepatica acutiloba*

The solitary blooms of the hepatica range in colour from a deep lavender blue to pale pink or white. Not until after these 1.2 to 2.5 cm. (½ to 1 in.) flowers have appeared do the new basal leaves develop. These leaves then remain intact until the following spring. A member of the buttercup family, the hepatica flowers in deciduous woods from March to June.

22 Autumn foliage, Moatfield Park ravine

23 PRAYING MANTIS *Mantis religiosa*

Originally from southern Europe, the praying mantis was accidentally brought to North America in 1899 on a commercial shipment of plants, and is now established in Ontario and the eastern United States. This 9 cm. (3½ in.) predator feeds on a variety of insects, including its own species—after mating, the female often devours her partner. The overwintering eggs hatch in late spring, and by early autumn the young have matured.

24 Ernest Thompson Seton Marsh in the fall

13 COMMON GRAY TREE FROG

14 LARGE-FLOWERED TRILLIUM

15 MOURNING CLOAK

16 BLACK-CAPPED CHICKADEE

17 POINTED BLUE-EYED GRASS

18 MISTY POND, BROOKBANKS RAVINE

19 GREAT BLUE HERON

20 BLUE FLAG

21 SHARP-LOBED HEPATICA

22 AUTUMN FOLIAGE, MOATFIELD PARK RAVINE

23 PRAYING MANTIS

24 ERNEST THOMPSON SETON MARSH IN THE FALL

Captions to plates 25–36

25–26 POLYPHEMUS MOTH *Antheraea polyphemus*

This large, night-flying moth is named after the one-eyed cyclops of Greek mythology, on account of the distinctive eye-spots on its hind wings. Like all giant silk-moths, the Polyphemus has no mouth-parts for feeding, and dies shortly after mating and egg-laying. The large green caterpillar feeds on various trees and shrubs, including oak, maple, and birch, until the pupa stage, when it spends the winter in a tough, leaf-wrapped cocoon. In the Toronto region, the adult is on the wing by early June.

27 LARGE YELLOW LADY'S SLIPPER
Cypripedium calceolus (see also plate 29)

The yellow lady's slipper blooms from May to July in bogs, swamps, marshes, and wet woods. Its yellow pouch resembles a slipper—hence not only the English, but the Latin name of this orchid. The large and small yellow lady's slippers are two varieties of the same species represented in the Toronto region. The smaller variety is distinguished by long purplish-brown lateral petals and a lip petal only 2 to 3.8 cm. (¾ to 1½ in.) long. By contrast, the large yellow lady's slipper has a lip petal 5 cm. (2 in.) long and twisted yellowish-green lateral petals. Both plants bear from three to five leaves with very pronounced parallel veins.

28 RED-WINGED BLACKBIRD *Agelaius phoeniceus*

One of the sounds of spring, the redwing's loud 'o-ka-leee' is first heard throughout marshy areas of Toronto in early March as the birds establish their territorial boundaries. As many as three broods of young may be raised each year. When the breeding season is finished the birds gather in large flocks in preparation for their autumn departure.

29 SMALL YELLOW LADY'S SLIPPER
Cypripedium parviflorum (see plate 27)

30–31 PAINTED LADY *Vanessa cardui*

Plate 30 shows an adult painted lady, or cosmopolite, emerging from the chrysalis. Possibly the most wide-spread butterfly in the world, this species is found in Africa, Europe, Indo-Australia, and North America. Like the monarch, it migrates south for the winter; however, the same adults do not undertake the return journey.

32 CREEPING BELLFLOWER
Campanula rapunculoides

A common garden species, this member of the bluebell family blossoms from July to September in fields and along roadsides throughout southern Canada. Standing 30 to 60 cm. (1 to 3 ft) tall, each stalk supports a single row of nodding, bell-shaped blooms.

33 FRINGED GENTIAN *Gentiana crinita*

The fringed gentian is one of the later bloomers in southern Ontario, flowering from late August to November in moist meadows and along seepage slopes. Opening only in bright sunlight, its four feathery petals quickly fold when the sky darkens. The colour of the tubular flowers, one or several of which may occur on a single plant, varies from pale to deep violet blue. Unfortunately this species is now rare in the Toronto region.

34 SPRING PEEPER *Hyla crucifer*

In early spring, Toronto's wetlands resound with the shrill call of this tiny 3.8 cm. (1½ in.) tree frog. The dark cross pattern on its back is distinctive, but the spring peeper is rarely seen except in the breeding season. After spending the summer in woodlands or marshes, it will winter in a crevice under a rock or log.

35 OYSTER MUSHROOM *Pleurotus ostreatus*

Resembling clusters of oyster-shells, layers of oyster mushrooms are found on both conifer and hardwood logs and stumps. The dull white fan-shaped cap, usually stalkless, exudes an appealing fruity fragrance, and is considered a choice edible.

36 DOWNY YELLOW VIOLET *Viola pubescens*

This attractive yellow violet, which grows to a height of 15 to 40 cm. (6 to 15¾ in.), blooms in May and June in the light shade of open woods. It is distinguished from other yellow violets by the downy hair on both the stem and the serrated, heart-shaped leaves. The small pansy-like flower is only 2 cm. (¾ in.) across.

25 POLYPHEMUS MOTH

26 POLYPHEMUS MOTH

27 LARGE YELLOW LADY'S SLIPPER

28 RED-WINGED BLACKBIRD

29 SMALL YELLOW LADY'S SLIPPER

30 PAINTED LADY

31 PAINTED LADY

32 CREEPING BELLFLOWER

33 FRINGED GENTIAN

34 SPRING PEEPER

35 OYSTER MUSHROOM

36 DOWNY YELLOW VIOLET

Captions to plates 37–48

37 WOODCHUCK *Marmota monax*

This large rodent, also known as the groundhog, averages 56 cm. (22 in.) in length and may weigh up to 5.8 kg. (13 lb.). Feeding on a variety of plants and grasses, it may be found in parks and ravines throughout Metro. An average of four young are born each spring; they often remain with their mother until the following year, spending the winter in hibernation. Legend has it that if, on the second day of February, an early-rising groundhog sees his shadow on leaving his den, forty more days of winter are to be expected.

38 SPRING BEAUTY *Claytonia virginica*

This appealing early spring perennial blooms in moist woodlands from March to May. Only 1.3 to 2 cm. (½ to ¾ in.) wide, the candy-striped flower stands on a stalk 15 to 30 cm. (6 to 12 in.) high. At the base of this stalk is an underground tuber—similar to a water chestnut—which was used as food by native people and early settlers.

39 EASTERN COTTONTAIL *Sylvilagus floridanus* (see also plate 89)

As a species, the cottontail is active all year round. Most individuals have a short lifespan; usually only one in twenty will survive a full year. Those that do survive may produce four or more litters of from two to eight young each. Born in a shallow nest lined with grass and fur, the young grow rapidly and are capable of breeding after just six months. Cottontails are mainly nocturnal, and spend most of the daylight hours asleep.

40 MUSKRAT *Ondatra zibethicus*

Found in marshes, streams, and lakes throughout North America, this shy relative of the beaver is regularly trapped for its fur. Although it usually constructs its own lodge or waterside burrow, some muskrats have been known to move into a beaver lodge and stay there alongside the beavers.

41 BLANDING'S TURTLE *Emydoidea blandingi*

A bright yellow throat and a hinged lower shell identify the Blanding's turtle. Averaging 20 cm. (8 in.) in length, it inhabits ponds, lakes, and, occasionally, marshes, where it feeds on worms, insects, and various plants. This endangered species is rare in the Toronto region.

42 WOOD FROG *Rana sylvatica*

The handsome wood frog breeds in woodland pools across Canada from May to July. Unlike most frogs, this species can often be seen some distance away from the water.

43 WHITE-TAIL DRAGONFLY *Plathemis lydia*

Found near ponds, streams, and marshes, the white-tail is 4.7 cm. (1⅞ in.) long and has a wingspan of up to 7.6 cm. (3 in.). Like all dragonflies, this species begins life as an aquatic nymph. When fully grown, it leaves the water and takes to the air in search of mosquitoes.

44 East Branch, Don River.

45 MIDLAND PAINTED TURTLE
Chrysemys picta marginata

The smooth-shelled painted turtle inhabits shallow weedy waters, where it feeds on frogs, crayfish, earthworms, and plants. Growing to a length of 14 cm. (5½ in.), it is a sociable species and may often be seen sharing a favourite sun-bathing spot with others of its kind.

46 MALLARD *Anas platyrhynchos*

This attractive 71 cm. (28 in.) duck is widely distributed, inhabiting North America, Europe, and Asia. Feeding on sedges, grasses, and weeds, it is commonly seen in many of Toronto's parks and ravines. Broods of about eight to ten young are raised each year, solely by the females, while the males gather in small flocks by themselves. Mallards are strong fliers, reaching speeds of up to thirty miles an hour during their autumn migration south.

47 West Don River Valley

48 RED ADMIRAL *Vanessa atalanta*

The red admiral is a familiar sight in the Toronto region from May to October. Its larva feeds on nettles, the leaves of which it draws together and fastens with silk to form a protective covering. Although some adults winter here, few survive, and it is the arrival of migrants from the south each spring that assures the species' continuance in this area.

Captions to plates 49–60

49 MOURNING DOVE *Zenaidura macroura*

Taking its name from its mournful call, this graceful dove nests throughout southern Canada, even in densely populated urban areas. Its habitat ranges from meadows and woodlots to city parks—any place that provides an abundance of weed-seeds. The species breeds twice each season, the female laying two pure white eggs in a shallow nest of twigs.

50 EASTERN GRAY SQUIRREL *Sciurus carolinensis*

A common year-round resident of Toronto's parks and ravines, the omnivorous gray squirrel enjoys a varied diet of fruits, nuts, seeds, mushrooms, insects and, occasionally, nestling birds. Two broods of two to five young each are raised in a hollow tree or leafy nest. Of these, some, especially in southeastern Canada, may be pure black.

51 AMERICAN ROBIN *Turdus migratorius*

The robin's distinctive rusty-red breast and 'cheerily' song make it instantly recognizable to almost everyone. In a well-constructed cup-shaped nest, the female incubates from three to five blue-green eggs; then both parents provide the rapidly growing fledglings with worms, insects, and fruit. Although it has traditionally been considered a harbinger of spring, the robin is now wintering here in increasing numbers, generally in sheltered swampy areas.

52 RING-NECKED PHEASANT CHICK
Phasianus colchicus

A native of Eurasia, introduced here in the nineteenth century, the ring-necked pheasant is now a permanent resident of fields, meadows, and woodland edges throughout southern Canada. The large, handsome male measures approximately 90 cm. (36 in.) long and has a long, tapered, sword-like tail. The female—neither so large nor so flamboyant—has a more subdued mottled-brown plumage. Hatched in a vegetation-lined depression on the ground, the partridge-like chicks feed primarily on insects for several weeks before adopting the adult diet of corn, grain, grass, and fruits.

53 RED-SPOTTED PURPLE *Basilarchia astyanax*

This attractive 7.6 to 8.6 cm. (3 to 3³/₈ in.) butterfly frequents open fields, woodlands and water edges. A member of the brush-footed family, it characteristically has short hairy forelegs that are useless for walking. Its coloration, which closely resembles that of the toxic pipevine swallowtail, provides effective protection from birds.

54 STRIPED SKUNK *Mephitis mephitis*

This slow-moving mammal would be easy prey without its unique method of self-defence. Named for the bold black-and-white markings that tell its enemies to stay away, the striped skunk is not easily provoked. When threatened, however, it will stamp its front paws as a warning before spraying the aggressor with a foul-smelling liquid called mecraptan—its aim is remarkably accurate for a distance of up to 3.6 metres (12 ft). Primarily nocturnal, skunks spend the day sleeping in communal dens; as many as fifteen individuals may share the same house for the winter.

55 WILD GINGER *Asarum canadense*

The peculiar flower of this plant is never conspicuous, for it grows very close to the ground. Appearing in April or May at the base of two broad heart-shaped leaves, the cup-shaped flower is 3.8 cm. (1½ in.) wide and has three three pointed lobes, each with a twisted tail. The tubular root of this plant, which has a strong ginger aroma, may be dried and ground for use as a spice, or boiled with sugar to make candy.

56 CANADIAN TOAD *Bufo hemiophrys*

This familiar species is often seen in Toronto gardens; however, like most amphibians, it breeds and lays its eggs in the water. The tadpoles develop rapidly and emerge on land within three months. Once mature they will reach a length of 7.6 cm. (3 in.). The 'warts' on its skin are actually poison glands, powerful enough to kill or at least sicken a predator. If a snake does attempt to eat a toad, the unwilling victim will swell itself up to avoid being swallowed and may actually drag the aggressor some distance until the reptile gives up in frustration.

57 EASTERN MILK SNAKE
Lampropeltis triangulum triangulum

A frequent visitor to mouse-filled barns, this attractive snake was once thought to milk the resident cows—hence its common name. In fact, mice account for up to seventy per cent of its diet, making the milk snake a considerable benefit to farmers. Because of its blotched pattern and habit of vibrating its tail when in danger, this constrictor is often mistaken for a rattlesnake. Although it has sharp teeth and can inflict a painful bite, it is not venomous, and kills larger prey by crushing it in its coils.

58 YELLOW FLAG *Iris pseudacorus*

This showy species was introduced from Europe as a cultivated garden plant. Now widely established in North America as a wildflower, it stands 60 to 90 cm. (2 to 3 ft) tall and bears one or more brilliant yellow flowers on its smooth, sturdy stalk. The long sword-like leaves, which rise from a basal cluster, are sometimes longer than the stem. Yellow flag decorates marshes, stream- and river-banks throughout the Toronto region from June to August.

59 EASTERN TIGER SWALLOWTAIL *Papilio glaucus*

One of our largest and best-known butterflies, the tiger swallowtail is a regular visitor to both wild and garden flowers. Its family, the 'Papilioidae', consists of over 600 species distributed world-wide. Feeding on wild cherry, birch, ash, and the like, the larva spins a mat of silk on the surface of a leaf, on which it rests.

60 SAW-WHET OWL *Aegolius acadicus*

Eastern Canada's smallest owl measures a mere 18 cm. (7 in.) in height. In the daytime it roosts in the dense cover of low wet woodlands, but with the approach of dusk the saw-whet begins its nightly search for mice, bats, insects, and small birds. A permanent resident across the southern portion of Canada, it nests in abandoned woodpecker holes. Its curious name is derived from the sound of one of its calls, which resembles the metallic drone of a grinding saw.

49 MOURNING DOVE

50 EASTERN GRAY SQUIRREL

51 AMERICAN ROBIN

52 RING-NECKED PHEASANT CHICK

53 RED-SPOTTED PURPLE

54 STRIPED SKUNK

55 WILD GINGER

56 CANADIAN TOAD

57 EASTERN MILK SNAKE

58 YELLOW FLAG

59 EASTERN TIGER SWALLOWTAIL

60 SAW-WHET OWL

Captions to plates 61–72

61 MICHIGAN LILY *Lilium michiganense*

Growing to an impressive height of up to 182 cm. (6 ft), this magnificent plant blooms in marshes, thickets, and wet meadows from June to July; sometimes as many as twenty flame-orange flowers are displayed on a single robust stalk. Unfortunately the Michigan lily is found in fewer and fewer places each year, and is now considered an endangered species.

62 BLACK SWALLOWTAIL *Papilio polyxenes*

The black swallowtail frequents open fields and meadows and is usually observed flying close to the ground in search of nectar. Ranging as far south as Mexico, in Canada this species is double-brooded, and lays its eggs on plants belonging to the carrot family, including parsley and dill. For this reason it is often attracted to cultivated gardens.

63 TROUT LILY *Erythronium americanum*

Sometimes known as the dogtooth violet, this species is actually a member of the lily family. The name trout lily is derived from the distinctive markings of its two shiny brown-mottled leaves, which resemble those of a brook trout. The graceful nodding flower blooms in early spring in woodlands from Ontario east to Nova Scotia and south as far as Georgia.

64 COMMON SNAPPING TURTLE *Chelydra serpentina serpentina*

Apparently as ill-tempered as its common name suggests, the snapping turtle may weigh up to 16 kg. (35 lb.) and measure 46 cm. (18 in.) or more. Its diet includes plants, fish, frogs, and, occasionally, waterfowl. Although the species spends most of its time in the water, in spring females leave to dig a nest and lay their eggs, covering them carefully with sand. When the young hatch, they dig their way out and head straight for water.

65 COMMON GARTER SNAKE *Thamnophis sirtalis*

Found across Canada in a wide variety of habitats, the garter snake does not lay eggs but gives live birth to a litter of as many as thirty young. Since no parental care is given, the young snakes soon learn to fend for themselves. Though harmless, this familiar species may emit a foul-smelling fluid if captured or threatened.

66 EVENING PRIMROSE *Oenothera biennis*

Quite common wherever there is dry soil and open waste space, this beautiful biennial may reach a height of 60 to 152 cm. (2 to 5 ft). Its flowers open in the late afternoon and close by noon the following day; throughout the summer nights, from June to September, moths are drawn by their lovely lemon fragrance. The root may be eaten if it is picked during the first year, before the plant blooms.

67 CRAYFISH *Oronectes immunis*

The freshwater lobster, or 'crawdad', is represented by nine species in eastern Canada. Nocturnal crustaceans, they survive on a varied diet of plant and animal matter. The species illustrated is usually found in stagnant ponds or slow-moving streams, and will burrow into the ground if its habitat dries up.

68 RED-SPOTTED NEWT
Diemictylus viridescens viridescens

Also known as the eastern newt, this pretty amphibian begins its life in the water as a gilled larva, which hatches in spring from a small egg laid in a quiet stream or pond. By late summer the larva loses its gills and heads for land, where it will live for up to three years. At this stage it is known as a red eft. Once more, the 7.6 to 10 cm. (3 to 4 in.) eft—now called a newt—changes its colour to green, then returns to the water, where it will breed and spend the rest of its life.

69 GREEN FROG TADPOLE *Rana clamitans*

The green frog inhabits the shallow fresh waters of lakes, ponds, creeks, and springs throughout eastern North America. Breeding from March to August, it lays its jelly-covered eggs in three or four small clutches. The newly hatched tadpoles are gill-breathing and feed solely on algae, but with maturity the hind legs appear, the tail is absorbed, and the mouthparts change. Once the forelegs develop, the froglet is now an air-breathing creature, ready to leave the water if it so desires. Despite the species' name, adults may range in colour from green to bronze or brown.

70 AMERICAN GOLDFINCH *Carduelis tristis*

The striking 'wild canary', as it is often called, is found throughout most of southern Canada. A late nester, it raises from four to five young in a thistledown-lined nest. The males lose their bright coloration with the approach of winter and become hard to distinguish from the duller females. Rather that migrating south, some flocks winter in the Toronto area, living on seeds supplied by alders and various cone-bearing trees, as well as backyard feeders.

71 CANADA GOOSE *Branta canadensis*

The familiar 'V' formation of Canada geese heading south in their annual fall migration is a sure sign of the changing season. Wintering in the southern United States and Mexico, by March or early April mated pairs (which usually remain together for life) return to their favourite nesting grounds, where they raise from four to six goslings. The family remains together as a group until the next spring. In the Toronto region vast numbers of these geese have become permanent residents, wintering along the lakefront.

72 PURPLE TRILLIUM *Trillium erectum*

The purple trillium blooms in humus-rich woods throughout Ontario, Quebec, and Nova Scotia from April to June. Rising above a whorl of three broad leaves supported by a slender stalk, its maroon flower has a foul smell which attracts the flies that serve as pollinators.

61 MICHIGAN LILY

62 BLACK SWALLOWTAIL

63 TROUT LILY

64 COMMON SNAPPING TURTLE

65 COMMON GARTER SNAKE

66 EVENING PRIMROSE

67 CRAYFISH

68 RED-SPOTTED NEWT

69 GREEN FROG TADPOLE

70 AMERICAN GOLDFINCH

71 CANADA GOOSE

72 PURPLE TRILLIUM

Captions to plates 73–84

73 Dawn, Wigmore Ravine

74 TWIN-SPOTTED SPHINX *Smerinthus geminatus*
Members of the sphinx moth family derive their name from the distinctive posture of the larval stage, when the stocky caterpillar is usually seen holding its front quarters erect. Flying only after dusk, the adult moth rests undetected in foliage during the day.

75 BALTIMORE *Euphydryas phaeton*
This small, 2.5 to 6 cm. (1 to 2½ in.) butterfly frequents wet meadows and woodlands and is seldom seen far from its host plant, a member of the snapdragon family called the turtlehead *(Chelone glabra)*, on which it lays its eggs in large clusters. Once the larvae hatch in spring, they live together in a communal web until, when partially grown, they become inactive in preparation for their winter hibernation. With the return of spring the caterpillars awaken and the cycle resumes. Although uncommon in Ontario, the Baltimore can be found in certain areas of Toronto.

76 BLUE JAY *Cyanocitta cristata*
A typical member of the crow family, the blue jay is loud, lively, and mischievous, except while nesting, at which time it is unusually quiet. In a bulky nest of twigs, moss, and grass, four-to-six brown-spotted eggs are incubated. Once the young mature, families band together, forming flocks which feed on fruits, nuts, grains, and insects. Although the brilliant blue adults can be seen throughout the winter, they do in fact migrate, shifting southward from their breeding grounds.

77 RING-BILLED GULL *Larus delawarensis*
The ring-billed gull is one of Toronto's most visible birds. By nature a voracious scavenger, it frequents shorelines, fields, and city dumps across southern Canada in search of insects, worms, refuse, and, occasionally, eggs. These prolific birds nest in large colonies, preferably on islands which are often shared with other similar species. Their ever-increasing numbers within the city should come as no surprise, since the Leslie Street Spit, or 'Eastern Headland', is now home to one of the largest nesting colonies in the Great Lakes region.

78 BLACK AND YELLOW ARGIOPE *Argiope aurantia*
Usually seen in the late summer and early fall, this common 'garden spider' is one of the most beautiful of all the 40,000 species of spiders recorded in Canada. Found in southern Ontario and throughout the United States, it feeds on the various insects that blunder into its web. This species attains a body length of over 2.5 cm. (1 in.).

79 BIRDSFOOT TREFOIL *Lotus corniculatus*
This originally European member of the pea family is a pasture plant much like clover. A low-lying plant, it has a long stem which hugs the ground, rooting itself at each node. From June to September its brilliant yellow flowers decorate fields and roadsides throughout North America. The species' common name is derived from the arrangement of its narrow brown seeds pods, which resemble a bird's foot.

80 Autumn reflections, Wilket Creek

81 VICEROY *Basilarchia archippus*

At first glance the 7.6 cm. (3 in.) viceroy looks like a small monarch butterfly (see plate 95). This resemblance is an advantage, since birds that have suffered ill effects attempting to eat the poisonous monarch will usually avoid the viceroy. Feeding mainly on willow, poplar, and aspen, the larvae cover themselves with leaves to hibernate until the new growth of spring, when they resume eating and continue their life cycle. A member of the 'Nymphalid' family, the viceroy is widely distributed throughout North America.

82 CLIMBING BITTERSWEET *Celastrus scandens*

A favourite addition to dried-flower arrangements, this distinctive woody vine is becoming rare in Toronto as a result of overpicking. Its small green flowers produce clusters of yellow-orange berries which ripen to a rosy-red by October. Climbing bittersweet grows in woods and along riverbanks.

83 Winter Pond, Mocassin Trail Park

84 COMMON BLUET *Enallagma ebrium*

Here shown imprisoned by a late summer frost, this particular damselfly later thawed and flew off. In the earlier nymph stage this species subsists on tiny aquatic organisms, but adults feed on other soft-bodied insects. No more than 5 cm. (2 in.) long, the common bluet is widely distributed throughout Canada and the United States.

73 DAWN, WIGMORE RAVINE

74 TWIN-SPOTTED SPHINX

75 BALTIMORE

76 BLUE JAY

77 RING-BILLED GULL

78 BLACK AND YELLOW ARGIOPE

79 BIRDSFOOT TREFOIL

80 AUTUMN REFLECTIONS, WILKET CREEK

81 VICEROY

82 CLIMBING BITTERSWEET

83 WINTER POND, MOCASSIN TRAIL PARK

84 COMMON BLUET

Captions to plates 85–96

85 RACCOON *Procyon lotor*

The raccoon is an extremely intelligent animal; in fact only a few species of monkey and porpoise are thought by scientists to be more intelligent. Surprisingly well-adapted to the urban environment, it is primarily nocturnal and thrives on a varied diet of insects, frogs, mice, fruit, and vegetables. The kits, which are born in April or May, will remain with their mother for a full year.

86–87 CECROPIA MOTH *Hyalophora cecropia*

Undoubtedly Toronto's grandest insect, the Cecropia, or robin, moth boasts a wingspan of up to 15 cm. (6 in.). After wintering as a pupa in a large silk cocoon, the adult emerges once the fresh leaves of early June have appeared. The male is easily identified by its long feathery antennae, which are sensitive enough to scent a female for a radius of up to 4.8 km. (3 miles). Adults of both sexes live only one week.

88 HERB ROBERT *Geranium robertianum*

Herb Robert can be seen in Toronto's ravines from May through November. Growing on a hairy stem up to 45 cm. (18 in.) long, its small deep-pink-striped flowers complement the intense green of the fern-like leaves. This delicate member of the geranium family grows in rocky woods and along shorelines from Manitoba to Newfoundland.

89 COTTONTAIL *Sylvilagus floridanus* (see plate 39)

90 WHITE ADMIRAL *Limentis arthemis*

Also known as the banded purple, this striking butterfly is often seen visiting flowers or sunning itself near the edge of a wooded area. Its partially grown larva spends the winter hibernating in a rolled-up leaf, which is referred to as a 'hibernaculum'. The population of this species fluctuates, and although it is never abundant, in some years the white admiral is relatively common in certain parts of Toronto.

91 WILD COLUMBINE *Aquilegia canadensis*

The fragile scarlet and yellow flowers of the wild columbine can be found blooming from April to June along sloping banks and in rocky woods. A member of the buttercup family, this perennial grows from an underground rootstalk. The columbine's sweet nectar is a favourite of hummingbirds.

92 FRAGRANT WATER-LILY *Nymphaea odorata*

Also known as the pond lily, this elegant aquatic plant flowers in the quiet waters of marshes, ponds, and lakes from June to September. The large blossom, which opens to the early morning sun and closes by noon, is anchored to the bottom by long rootstalks. Fish and mammals feed on the fruit, which ripens underwater, while frogs and insects often rest on the floating leaves.

93 MUTE SWAN *Cygnus olor*

The mute swan, a native of Eurasia, is believed to have come north from New York State as an escaped species, and now lives in Ontario in a semi-wild condition. First reported along the Toronto region's waterfront in 1961, it is now wintering here in steadily increasing numbers. Although generally silent enough to merit its name, the mute swan will occasionally grunt or hiss.

94 Fall Foliage, Eastern Don

95 MONARCH *Danaus plexippus*

The monarch, or 'King Billy', is world-renowned not only for its beauty, but for its unique life-cycle. After hatching in the southern United States, millions of monarchs head northward each year, their offspring arriving in Toronto by the middle of June. Laying their eggs on milkweed plants, they may produce two or three broods in a season. Then, with the approach of autumn, they begin to gather in great numbers for their southern migration. Amazingly, this new generation follows the same route south, congregating at night on the same trees, and arriving at the same wintering grounds as did the previous years' migrants—though not one of them has ever made the journey before. After migrating 3000 km. (2000 miles) or more, they finally come to rest in Florida, California, or Mexico.

96 Sunrise on Lake Ontario

85 RACCOON

86 CECROPIA MOTH

87 CECROPIA MOTH

88 HERB ROBERT

89 COTTONTAIL

90 WHITE ADMIRAL

91 WILD COLUMBINE

92 FRAGRANT WATER-LILY

93 MUTE SWAN

94 FALL FOLIAGE, EASTERN DON

95 MONARCH

96 SUNRISE ON LAKE ONTARIO

Bibliography

Baillie, James L. 'A Century of Change—Birds'. *Ontario Naturalist* 5, no. 3 (September 1967).

Barnett, J.M. 'Ashbridge's Bay'. *Ontario Naturalist*, December 1971.

Behler, John L., and F. Wayne King. *The Audubon Society Field Guide to North American Reptiles and Amphibians*. New York: Alfred A. Knopf Inc., 1979.

Berchem, F.R. *The Yonge Street Story*. Toronto: McGraw-Hill Ryerson Ltd., 1977.

Bigelow, Howard Elson. *Mushroom Pocket Field Guide*. New York: Macmillan Pub. Co. Inc., 1974.

Bonis, Robert R. *A History of Scarborough*. Scarborough Public Library, 1968.

Bull, John, and John Farrand Jr. *The Audubon Society Field Guide to North American Birds (Eastern Region)*. New York: Alfred A. Knopf Inc., 1977.

Cahalane, Victor H. *Mammals of North America*. New York: Macmillan Pub. Co. Inc., 1958.

Chapman, L.J., and D.F. Putnam. *The Physiography of Southern Ontario*, 2nd ed. Toronto: University of Toronto Press, 1966.

Checklist of Plants in Four Toronto Parks. Toronto Field Naturalists' Club, 1972.

Clement, Roland C. *The Living World of Audubon*. New York: Grosset and Dunlap Inc., 1974.

Conant, Roger. *A Field Guide to Reptiles and Amphibians of Eastern North America*. Boston: Houghton Mifflin Co., 1958.

Concept and Objectives of M.T.P.D. Toronto: Metropolitan Toronto Planning Dept., 1976.

Crocker, Denton W., and David W. Barr. *Handbook of the Crayfishes of Ontario*. Toronto: University of Toronto Press, 1968.

Everett, Thomas H. *The New York Botanical Garden Illustrated Encyclopedia of Horticulture*, vol. 2. New York: Garland Publishing Inc., 1981.

Faull, J.H. *The Natural History of the Toronto Region, Ontario, Canada*. Toronto: The Canadian Institute, 1913.

Ferguson, Mary, and Richard Saunders. *Canadian Wildflowers*. Toronto: Van Nostrand Reinhold Ltd., 1976.

Freeman, E.B. *Toronto's Geological Past: An Introduction*. Ontario Division of Mines, 1976.

Froom, Barbara. *The Snakes of Canada*. Toronto: McClelland and Stewart Ltd., 1972.

Gilbertson, Forbes. 'The Don: An Urban River Struggling for Survival'. *Canadian Geographical Journal*, February 1972.

Gingrich, John. *Bird Migration Chart*. Toronto Field Naturalists' Club, April 1968.

Godfrey, W. Earl. *The Birds of Canada*. Ottawa: Queen's Printer, 1966.

Goodwin, Clive E. *A Bird-Finding Guide to the Toronto Region*. Toronto Field Naturalists' Club, 1979.

Guillet, Edwin C. *Early Life in Upper Canada*. Toronto: The Ontario Publishing Co., Ltd., 1933.

Hart, Patricia W. *Pioneering in North York: A History of the Township*. Toronto: General Publishing Co., Ltd., 1968.

Hounsom, Eric W. *Toronto in 1810*. Toronto: Coles Publishing Co., 1975.

Iden, Peter. *Toronto Bird-Finding Guide*. Toronto Field Naturalists' Club, 1967.

Judd, W.W., and J.M. Speirs. *A Naturalist's Guide to Ontario*. Toronto: University of Toronto Press, 1964.

Karrow, P.F. *Geological Association of Canada: Proceedings 20*. Toronto: Geological Association of Canada, 1969.

Kosch, Alois. *The Young Specialist Looks at Wildflowers*. London: Burke Publishing Co. Ltd., 1964.

Lamont, Graham. *Toronto and York County: A Sample Study*. Toronto: J.M. Dent and Sons Canada Ltd., 1970.

Lansdowne, J. Fenwick, and John A. Livingston. *Birds of the Eastern Forest*, 2 vols. Toronto: McClelland and Stewart Ltd., 1968, 1970.

Lizars, K.M. *The Valley of the Humber*. Toronto: William Briggs, 1913.

Marvels and Mysteries of our Animal World. New York: Reader's Digest Association, Inc., 1964.

Metropolitan Toronto Parks: A Compendium. Toronto: Metropolitan Parks Dept., January 1977.

Metropolitan Toronto Valleyland Study. Toronto: Metropolitan Toronto Planning Dept., May 1976.

Miller, Orson K. Jr. *Mushrooms of North America*. New York: E.P. Dutton and Co. Inc., 1979.

Milne, Lorus Johnson. *The Audubon Society Field Guide to North American Insects and Spiders*. New York: Random House, 1980.

Mulvany, C. Pelham. *Toronto Past and Present: A Handbook of the City*. Toronto: W.E. Caiger, 1884.

Niering, William J., and Nancy C. Olmstead. *The Audubon Society Field Guide to North American Wildflowers (Eastern Region)*. New York: Alfred A. Knopf Inc., 1979.

Outdoors Canada. The Reader's Digest Association (Canada) Ltd., 1977.

Parker, Bruce. 'Naturalized Birds in the Toronto Region'. *Toronto Field Naturalists' Newsletter* 352 (December 1982).

Peterson, Roger Tory. *A Field Guide to the Birds (Eastern Region)*. Boston: Houghton Mifflin Co., 1978.

Pile, Robert Michael. *The Audubon Society Field Guide to North American Butterflies*. New York: Alfred A. Knopf Inc., 1981.

Reid, R. 'What's Happening with Wetlands in Ontario?' *Ontario Naturalist*, Summer 1979.

Sauriol, Charles. *Remembering the Don*. Toronto: Consolidated Amethyst Communications Inc., 1981.

Scadding, Henry. *Toronto of Old*. Toronto: Oxford University Press, 1966.

Sedgwick, D. 'The Spit'. *Seasons*, Spring 1980.

Smith, Hobart M. *Amphibians of North America*. Racine, Wisc.: Western Publishing Co. Inc., 1978.

Spelt, Jacob. *Toronto*. Toronto: Collier-Macmillan Canada, Ltd., 1973.

Stanek, V.J. *The Illustrated Encyclopedia of Butterflies and Moths*. London: Octopus Books, Ltd., 1977.

Toronto Field Naturalists' Club Ravine Surveys: 'Chatsworth Ravine' (1973); Brookbanks (1974); Chapman Creek' (1975); Wigmore Park (1975); Park Drive' (1976); 'Burk Ravine' (1977); 'Taylor Creek—Woodbine Bridge' (1976); 'West Don River Valley' (1978).

Toronto the Green. Toronto Field Naturalists' Club, 1976.

Toronto Island Public School. *A History of the Toronto Islands*. Toronto: The Coach House Press, 1972.

Walker, Frank N. *Sketches of Old Toronto*. Toronto: Longman's Canada Ltd., 1965.

West, Bruce. *Toronto* (The Romance of Canadian Cities Series). Toronto: Doubleday Canada Ltd., 1979.

Wetmore, Alexander. *Song and Garden Birds of North America*. Washington, D.C.: National Geographic Society, 1964.

Whitaker, John O., Jr. *The Audubon Society Field Guide To North American Mammals*. New York: Alfred A. Knopf Inc., 1980.

Index of Plates